# Iaroslav Wise

# Move Mountains

This book, unlike some other books, instead of teaching a particular skill (e.g. how to be a good accountant, how to drive a car, how to run a business, etc.) helps develop the attitude for accomplishing any good undertaking, including studying and working. This is important in the modern world where people encounter all kinds of obstacles and sometimes all that they need is a reminder about God's love, the importance of courage in achieving positive results and how to be happy. The title of this book is inspired by Mt 17:20 and Mk 11: 23 (the Bible).

Wise, I. (2021). *Move mountains*. Calgary, AB: Edocation Corp.

**ISBN 978-1-989531-26-6**

| | |
|---|---|
| Format: | Book (hardcover) |
| Language: | English |
| Written & designed by: | Iaroslav Wise |
| Published by: | Edocation Corp. |
| Disclaimer: | This book is published as has been submitted by the author and in the original language |

# Acknowledgements

Thank God.

Thank you to my family for taking on a lot of day-to-day tasks which allowed me to complete the work.

Thank you to you, the reader, for using this book!

# How to use this book

Unlike some other books, for example, novels, this book is intended for "sprint readers" – readers do not need to read a whole chapter of the book at a time or to read it from the very beginning through the middle to the end; instead, any time a reader feels that s/he would appreciate a word of support, cheer or wisdom, s/he can open the book and read one or more poems. Even after reading the whole book, readers may find it useful to come back and reread some of it again from time to time.

Alternatively, readers can read the poems by category (e.g. "Thanksgiving", "Love", "Happiness", etc.) or find the key words (e.g. 'hope', 'life', 'smile', etc.) they are interested in at the end of the book, in the "Index (tags)" section. Readers are welcome to highlight, underline, otherwise mark any poems they like and make notes in the corresponding section at the end of the book.

If you have found a poem which you would like to share with your family, friends or colleagues feel free to do so (please, quote) by sending such a poem to them, by lending them the book or by purchasing a new book for them as a gift.

# Table of contents

ix

xi

xiii

# THANKSGIVING

## Do good without expecting any praise

Do good without expecting any praise;
Do good for the good's sake.
No gratitude? Don't even gaze,
Just give without expecting to take.

One day Christ healed ten lepers*, ten,
But only one came back to thank.
So, why should we expect it then?
No doubt, you'll be given your due,
If not here and now, it's even better.
Each day brings in something new.
This poem is an open letter.

* See also Lk. 17:11-19.

*Saturday – Sunday 05–06.05.2007*


## Thank You, Father, for the success

Thank You, Father, for the success in studies and science!
On You I have fixed my strong reliance,
And all worked out well for me, Your slave,
Much better than expected and You taught me to be brave!

*Sunday 09.06.2013*

## With You

I relied on You and won,
You gave a victory again,
Because You are the Only One.
Your Love cannot be vain!

You are the Loving God!
You are Gracious indeed.
You help people a lot;
With You, we won't be in need!

*Wednesday 05.10.2011*


## Oh Lord, thank You for the people who help even strangers

Oh Lord, thank You for the people who help even strangers,
Who are not afraid of consequences.
They are not strong rangers,
But their true love is the same in all consequences.

*Sunday 31.07.2011*


## Oh God, I see your blessing everywhere

Oh God, I see your blessing everywhere:
In humans, plants and animals, including a bear.
Thank You, Father, for Your unconditional Love.
Always send it to us like a dove!

*Sunday 19.08.2012*

## Kind people

Kind people will save the world.
Their heart warmth will warm in winter,
Their kindness will rid of a splinter;
From a cold will heal their word.

When one of them will help you –
This, be sure, will happen –
Tell them "thank you!"
And keep it in heart to someone to return.

*Friday 18.03.2011*


## Let Your Holy Name be praised

Let Your Holy Name be praised,
How sweet are Your laws!
Let the world be amazed,
Strong health and high spirits they cause.

How wonderful they are for all!
Only You give breath, abundant life
In winter and summer, in spring and in fall.
You reinforce me in a strife.

You give for free,
And I do thrive,
Like a young showing-green tree.
You prepare a Wonderful Place for us to arrive.

You send comfort, release
And watch, and help on every step, <u>for good</u>.

Thank You for love and friends, for bread and peace.
Thank You for life, I simply conclude.

*Tuesday 03.02.2009*


## Do not hope to earn back more

Do not hope to earn back more,
Do good.
This is of righteousness store,
This is for soul delicious food.

Do not expect to hear thanks:
God sees you anyway.
Too busy are people of high ranks.
You do good and pray.

*Thursday 23.06.2011*


## Thank Thee, Father, for Thy Love

Thy Love comes and revives me.
I was suppressed and sad,
But Thou gave me Thy support
And made Thy slave as strong as a fort!

My spirit rejoiced!
And I thanked Thee, glorified Thy Name!
I was wrong…
But Thou treated me with Love along!

*Tuesday – Wednesday 29–30.05.2012*

## Plans

What I have planned did not happen, you know.
All week is like this, so what's wrong?
On the roads I planned, I didn't go,
But still I hoped for better – didn't have to for long

Because better did happen, it's true.
Thank Thee, Father, for now I see.
The clouds are white and the sky is blue.
Thank Thee for I am healthy and free!

*Thursday 25.12.2008*


## To a faithful person

Thank God for all achievements
For it is He Who sends all good things:
Health, food, friendly agreements;
Discoveries for scientists, prosperity for kings.

What can you do?
You can pray and not get stressed,
Your heart is right, your faith is true!
Your head is bright, soon you'll get some rest.

*Sunday 09.06.2013*

# Let the Name of God be blessed now and forever!

Let the Name of God be blessed now and forever!
Let us sing to Him all who is clever!
He blesses those who love Him truly,
He makes them happy and cures them fully!

*Sunday 12.05.2013*

# God gives all (1)

God gives all:
Happiness and health,
With or without wealth;
He also hears when you call.

Be brave, He is with you.
Do good and live.
The time is short, the days are few.
Be brave and wise, when your hand is able – give.

*Sunday 09.01.2010*

# Be thankful whatsoever

Be thankful whatsoever –
This is the start to be clever.
Praise God with love in heart –
This is a reliable port to depart.

In all you do, have faith:
It will take you to your place.
You and yours will thrive;
In a beautiful land you will arrive.

*Sunday 11.11.2012*


## God is my Strength

God is my Strength –
Throughout the length
Of my days –
He is the Source of my praise.

*Thursday 02.01.2020*


## God is my shield

God is my shield –
Whom shall I fear?
In the air, on the sea, on a field
He is the One Who makes my way and mind clear.

I call on Him each day
And during distress
He spreads His wings over me on every way.
In Him, I will rejoice; Him will I confess.

*Wednesday 06.11.2019*

## 2nd chance

When you get a second chance
In a worthy enterprise, studies, dance,
Use it wisely, thankfully; appreciate.
A third chance may be too late.

*Sunday 17.11.2019*


## Glorify God and do not fear

Glorify God and do not fear;
Toward wisdom and faith incline your ear.
Let your deeds be sincere and bold;
Be careful and protect what you hold.

*Saturday 30.11.2019*


## Thank You, Father, for this event

Thank You, Father, for this wonderful event!
You do better than my best intent.
You give generously without asking back.
You are the Source That gives without lack.

*Thursday – Monday 06-10.10.2011*

# How much I've been given!

How much I've been given!
Thank Thee, Father, for all!
To juicy meadows I've been driven.
You prevented me from my fall.

How can I stumble
If on God my hope I fix?
Those who love, believe and are humble,
They are building their house on stone, of bricks.

He always sees what we need,
God takes care of us all, even a dove.
So, I will not lean on a man, on a reed.
Thank Thee for Thy wonderful love!

*Monday 06.11.2006*


# The Eucharist is always something more

The Eucharist* is always something more
Than my mind can draw.
The Father Himself opens the saving door
And your soul will never be like a weak straw.

* Gr. (εὐχαριστία) literally meaning "thanksgiving" and is used
as a synonym for Communion (Ukr. *Причастя*).

*Wednesday 05.06.2013*

## My God is my Saviour

I thought that I had lost,
But You changed my losses
Into victories of precious cost.
And my foot safely crosses

On an invisible bridge
That only You have spread,
On a ridge…
In peace, Your servant eats his bread!

Thank You, Father!

*Sunday 11.03.2012*

# LOVE

## Love God and believe (1)

Love God, He loved you from the start.
Love God with all your heart!
Believe, God exists, indeed,
He helps in every kind deed!

*Sunday 16.02.2014*

## Let us love God with all our heart!

Let us love God with all our heart!
Let us love our neighbour!
Let us be faithful and not depart.
This will bring us success in our labour!

*Sunday 27.10.2013*

## Keep in touch with your family

When all is well, we can get by on our own;
When times are rough,
We do not want to be alone –
We seek our family and our issues diminish by half.

Therefore, make sure you are always in touch
For your and their sake.
Your time with them does not have to be much,
Just let it be true and quality – let it not be fake.

*Saturday 21.11.2020*

## Nothing can separate you from His love

Love God with all your heart.
Nothing can separate you from His love:
Neither abyss nor height, neither end nor start.
Elevate your heart like a dove!
Let not food or anything else interfere.
Be strong, give up your fear.
Remember, man cannot prevail over your soul.
Be wise, seek God and you will achieve your goal!

*Sunday 19.05.2013*

## Love fully

Love God with all your heart!
Let it be fully, not in part!
For God wants this.
Open your ears in order not to miss!

*Sunday 26.05.2013*

## I live with love

My heart is burning,
I am alive.
My brain is learning.
What a drive!

I am a living creature,
This is my feature.

It's like a dove,
I win with love!

*Friday – Sunday 11–13.06.2010*

## My dog is my treasure

My dog is my treasure:
He takes me for a walk for health and for pleasure.
He is the best alarm of all time:
He prevents mischief and a crime.

He loves his "pack",
His loyalty will never lack.
My dog is big on cheer.
He is smart and that is clear.

*Sunday 04.10.2020*

## Jesus Christ – my Hope

In Christ alone
My hope is fixed.
My heart won't moan,
He bestows His Grace upon all nations mixed!

He is my Day!
He is my Light!
He is the Truth that words of love and wisdom say.
He is my Breath, my Hope, my Sight!

Oh Jesus Christ!
Thank You for life,
Thank You for love!
The Only begotten Son of God, oh Christ!

**Refrain**
To the peoples of every race
He grants His Grace,
To the small and big among His friends.
His love extends beyond the world's ends!

*Tuesday 08.11.2011*


## Your smile is light

Your smile is light,
Your eyes are pure springs.
Your soul is bright.
You add me wings.

*Wednesday 30.06.2010*


## Love God and believe (2)

Love God and believe,
What you are asking, you will receive.
But "purchase" patience and keep, –
It is time to work, not to sleep.

*Sunday 28.03.2013*

## Stick to love

Stick to love and do all things
With it indeed:
Working, studying, curing stings,
Resting, waiting, taking lead…

Let God deal
With the things they do.
You stick to what is true
Heeding to the loving, wise and courageous appeal.

*Sunday 16.08.2020*


## Love God and act according to this!

Love God and act according to this!
In order to catch up and not to miss,
In order to win and not to lose,
In order to keep stable in the cruise!

*Sunday 01.12.2013*


## Love God to fulfill His commandments

Love God to fulfill His commandments
To help your neighbour,
To improve your life by introducing certain amendments;
To make successful all, including your labour.

The things will improve, believe.
Trust in God and go!
With His help, you will, certainly, achieve.
May love help you plant many good seeds for a generous
harvest to mow.

*Monday – Saturday 9–21.12.2013*


## While we still have the loving ones around

While we still have the loving ones around,
Let us be thankful, loving, let us appreciate.
Let our words be cheerful; hearts – hopeful; judgement – sound.
Let's say the kind words before it is too late.

*Friday 10.07.2020*


## You say a lot when you say nothing at all

You say a lot when you say nothing at all:
Your eyes are a thousand-page book,
Deeper than Niagara Fall;
Truthful is your look.

*Sunday 07.11.2010*

## I love God

I love God with all my heart,
Him, Who loved me from the start!
He blessed me with success!
I prayed to God and He gave me more, not less!

My soul, rejoice in God all days!
My tongue, pronounce!
Let the Name of God be blessed!
Let the thankful songs be sung with zest!

*Saturday 23.03.2013*

## Faith and hope

Reinforce your faith and hope
In order to stay focused on your scope.
Small things distract us,
But let us avoid fuss.

Believe, your Defender is Strong!
Your trouble will not last long –
The victory is close to you.
Remain in love that is true.

*Sunday 27.01.2013*

# Love God with all your heart! (1)

Love God with all your heart!
Be thankful for what you possess,
From here start
If you want to get more, not less.

*Sunday 05.08.2012*


# Education for children

Educate your children, friend,
To love God and to respect their family truly,
To know what to do with a bully,
To persist in good and to amend.

Explain and work on them day and night.
Do not be shy to say "no", but explain why.
Be loving, but consistent even if they cry.
Spend time on them, teach them to grow in light.

*Thursday 05.03.2020*


# Do all things with love

Do all things with love.
Doubt not about doing kind things.
Let your heart whirl up like a dove.
Kind things are glory for kings.

*June 2014*

# Love God with all your heart (1)

Love God with all your heart;
Love your neighbour as yourself, indeed.
Christ is our Door and our Start.
Let our love be manifest in word and deed.

*Sunday 29.12.2013*


# Love God with all your mind

Love God with all your mind,
But don't let your love be hypothetical or blind:
Show your love in deeds –
Help your neighbour in his needs!

*Sunday 06.10.2013*


# God loves me, it's true

God loves me, it's true.
God gives much more than I deserve:
I am like a fresh flower under the dew.
To gain and not to lose I have the commandments to observe.

All I need is a faithful love,
And that is the law.
It is so mighty, but is more gentle than a dove;
We are to give it, but we are not to keep it in store.

*Monday – Tuesday 26-27.02.2007*

## Whatever happens, stick together

Whatever happens, stick together,
You are one team in spite of any weather.
Forget all the quarrels at once and forever,
Forgive and live because you are clever.

The power is in the unity.
It's not my idea –
It is an unwritten law of the community.
Be brave to face it, you need no fear.

Let us swim together
And we'll support each other,
Your burden will seem a feather!
I am the luckiest man to have a sister, to have a brother!

*Tuesday 20.02.2007*


## Loving animals

Loving animals is the thing to teach your children duly.
In return, the animals will be loving and devoted fully –
This is true for domestic creatures, –
With wild ones, caution and respect are the required features.

*Sunday 15.03.2020*

## Space in heart

My heart is spacious for God,
But other people may find it tight.
Yet, if their heart is just as light,
They, too, will find it spacious, loving and bright.

*Tuesday 17.03.2020*


## Love God like He has loved us

Love God like He has loved us;
Forgive people as He forgives to you.
Be kind on foot, in a car, on a bus.
The darkest hour is before the morning dew.
So, keep your faith which is true.
Don't stop believing!
You will break through
Because truly God loves you!

*Sunday 07.07.2013*


## With all your heart

Love God with all your heart!
Trust your ways to Him, be smart!
You will look and will be surprised
When all your plans turn out realized.

Rely on God, be strong!
Have patience, it won't take long:

The solution is near!
Hold faith; the things will soon be clear!

*Sunday – Monday 28-29.04.2013*

## You are the flower

You are the flower
Let God be your Tower.
Let coldness of winter not freeze you.
Let your feet be washed with crystal clear dew!

*Sunday 10.03.2013*

## Love above all

Wherever you go, you are with me.
Distance is relative, and so is time.
You and I are free.
About love is this rhyme.

Everything is possible for us
As long as our hearts beat with love.
Sad and boring is fuss –
Spread your wings and fly like a dove.

Let kind deeds speak.
Remain true in any weather.
Love is strong; hesitation and fear are weak.
Although far – we are together.

*Friday 02.01.2009*

## I appreciate your love

I know, God hears your prayer.
I like your bright eyes, your hair,
Your smile, kind heart –
I love all of you, not just a part!

Thank you for your love and support!
Our friendship is my safe port.
Your advice makes difficulties a feather.
I want us to be together.

*Sunday 28.07.2013*


## Our love

Love is what I have to share;
Love is what to me is dear.
My love to you I hereby do declare.
Be my wife for your love in front of me to glare.

*Sunday 02.02.2020*


## How to perform great feats

Your deeds don't have to be big to be great –
Just try to avoid being late;
Say "thank you", "sorry" when needed;
Be loving, helpful and mean it.

*Saturday 25.11.2012*

## What is trending now?

What is trending now?
It's love – it was and always will be.
Therefore, follow it – with respect, courage, patience – this is how.
Keep your heart and mind free.

*Monday 04.11.2019*


## Let no one doubt

Let no one doubt
When they donate
A good deed, a piece of worthy advice, a trout,
A loving word to extinguish hate

And let no one criticize
A good, needed intention –
Instead, let them support, be wise;
Let us be courageous and pay attention.

*Thursday – Saturday 02-04.01.2020*


## Love God with all your heart! (2)

Love God with all your heart!
He loved you first from the start.
Do for your neighbour
Good favour, as good service as your own labour.

Love God with all your thought!
Remember how devotedly for you He fought.
Eat you bread;
Do not be jealous, be thankful instead.

*Sunday 17.06.2012*


## Let us love God

Let us love God, my brother!
Let us love God, my sister!
Let us respect our father and mother;
Let's be polite to our boss, that solid mister.

Help your neighbour
To cope with his labour.
Be gentle always and serious at times!
I have prepared for you these simple rhymes.

*Sunday 16.09.2012*


## If you love, be worthy of it

If you love, be worthy of it:
Show your strength, faith, wit.
May God also send you wisdom to choose
To find yourself and the friend and not to lose.

*Sunday 27.10.2019*

## Sainthood call

Let your light shine
Before people truly
Who fast and who dine
That they may rejoice fully;

That they should glorify
Our God – the Creator of all;
That they, too, may find the will and desire to try;
That they may discover their sainthood call.

*Monday 16.09.2019*

## Banff

Have you been to Banff ever?
Going there may be clever:
This beauty reminds
Of the Creator's love and sets free our minds.

*Wednesday 28.08.2019*

## Do all things with love sincere

Do all things with love sincere:
You will go far, you won't go near;
You will improve the world around you;
Your light will shine to others, true.

*Monday 12.08.2019*

# Love God with all your heart (3)

Love God with all your heart,
Be frank in it: in whole, in part.
You will see the way!
God will show, so love and pray.

Love in word and love in deed
For love is dead without good seeds.
So many brothers are in need,
Look at your neighbour, his poverty pleads.

Love God and remember:
From January through December,
From morning till night,
Let your love shine, let love be bright!

*Sunday 29.08.2010*


# Love story

You were several years younger
And I was so naive.
We met at the fishmonger's,
You were about to leave.

I asked how the selection was that day.
You smiled and said what you liked.
You explained the best cooking way,
It was trout or pike.

You gave me your email
In case I forgot how.

Since then we often met; we often pray like in a fairy tale,
We've been married for twelve years now.

*Saturday – Monday 04-06.03.2017*


## Your eyes are deeper than Moraine Lake

Your eyes are deeper than Moraine Lake,
Your voice is more tender than the wave of the sea.
Your smile makes my sadness flake;
A talk with you is like a refreshing shade of a tree.

Your hair is softer than silk;
Your "hi" is reviving.
Your skin is milder than milk;
Your love is worth surviving.

I thank God that above all you are my friend.
We are as we are, we do not pretend.

*Sunday 31.07.2011*


## Giving birth to children

Giving birth to children, friend,
Has never been about money –
It has always been about love you send,
Not about an extra mouth to take away "your" honey.

Thus, it's not about money to support –
It is about love to give.

If you have love, never fear to give birth to whole cohort.
If you lack love, it's better if by yourself you live.

*Monday 06.05.2019*


## The real wealth

Children are the real wealth!
In your older years they will add to your health.
Against evil people they will protect.
And new technologies for you they will select.

*Thursday 28.02.2013*

# HAPPINESS

## When you want to pray

When you want to pray,
Do, do not delay.
Let your prayer be from your heart;
It does not have to be long, loud or any complex art.

*Thursday 10.12.2020*


## Once upon a time there was an oak

Once upon a time there was an oak
Which was not afraid of the boldest stroke.
It grew in the heart of a wood, –
But now you will not find the place where it stood.

Lightnings struck it several times,
But after this it saw a lot of primes.
One day the wood caught fire,
But the tree lived on like a strong desire.

Every beast and bird admired its power;
Supported and watered by its friend, shower…
Nobody knew where the termites had come from:
They consumed the tree faster than any storm.

People often stand bad privations
Keeping themselves away from temptations.
They are brave and are not afraid of rifles.
Do they have to dissipate their energies on trifles?

*Thursday 07.07.2005*

# How obscure tomorrow is

How obscure tomorrow is.
It's useless to try,
But people often strive to please
That day; oh, poor thing, poor guy!

Others suffer living too:
They have adopted the faded day,
Yesterday it's called, it's true.
What else should I say?

It's worth watching our own step,
Whatever we do, we live today.
Vanity is a real trap.
Adopt wisdom and ask it to stay.

*Monday – Tuesday 12–13.02.2007*


# So much I have, indeed

So much I have, indeed,
But still for love I feel such greed;
Always want praise
And nothing except sunny days...

I also dislike making mistakes,
But they are as plenty as water in lakes.
All seems to be wrong,
Always unhappy and displeased is my song...

And it is not right.
To be happy means to fight,

To fight silly ambitions and pride.
Moaning is narrow; solutions are wide!

So, be happy, my soul!
You will praise God for every goal.
Be thankful and strive if you want more.
He enters who knocks at a door!

*Monday 21.04.2008*

## Let life be present

Love God with all your heart;
Be kind, gracious and smart.
Let life be present in you;
Let your faith be true!

*Sunday 30.06.2013*

## Have you ever felt lonely?

Have you ever felt lonely?
So have I,
But we aren't the only.
Weren't there tears in every eye?

Look around,
Do not concentrate on yourself, try.
You'll hear a calm sound –
The poor cry.

They suffer, but never moan,
They have the right, but – no.
Their faith is a stone;
Their love is brighter than snow.

*Monday – Tuesday 04–05.06.2007*


## Rich people are rarely happy

He has a lot of money,
But can he use his wealth?
Any time he can afford eating honey,
But for this he has no health.

He has become rich,
But has he become happy?
He can buy all to fill his fridge,
But in love and Life, will he stand snappy?

*Sunday 11.08.2013*


## Amendments, light & cheer

It's never too late to amend;
To change to a better trend,
To sail courageously to light
And to keep cheer, faith, hope and love in sight.

*Friday 16.10.2020*

# Count it joy

When trials and temptations
Come along,
Count it joy enduring with patience –
For those do not last long;

But the reward is great
To those who sustain with faith;
Therefore, be thankful for what's on your plate;
Rejoice, pray, create.

\* See also Jam. 1:2-5.

*Saturday 10.10.2020*


# Rejoice in God and thank for all

Rejoice in God and thank for all.
Abide in peace, abandon fear
And let the sky above for you be clear.
Have faith and pray, pursue your dreams, both big and small!

*Pascha Monday 21.04.2011*


# Do charity

Do charity not in front of people, but in the secrecy of your
heart.
Help people when they need your help;

Today is the best day to start.
Do it in silence, not with a yelp.

## Trust in God and worry not

Trust in God and worry not:
He is the One Who save you out of the cold and hot.
When all is quiet, and when things are rough,
Act with faith and find time to laugh.

*Sunday 19.07.2020*


## Love life

Love life to appreciate
Every moment, everyone, every situation;
To be wise, to act boldly and not to be late;
To be thankful, loving; to do good with determination.

*Friday 10.07.2020*


## Timely

When we are able to perform a kind deed,
We must do so timely, and that's the key:
To donate, repent, abandon greed,
Say loving words, support, foresee.

*Friday 10.07.2020*

# Do not lose hope, my friend

Do not lose hope, my friend,
Find strength to be consistent.
Bad things will end;
Wins he who is insistent.

Think not what others will think:
Think of life eternal.
Opinions change in a wink.
Remain in love and peace internal.

*Thursday 05.05.2011*


# Doctor Diet, Doctor Quiet & Doctor Merryman

Buddy, if you are tired,
Try Swift's Dr. Diet, Dr. Quiet and Dr. Merryman
To ensure that you work steady and are not fired;
That for your healthy, happy life you have a plan.

*Sunday 21.06.2020*


# Trust in God and do not worry

Trust in God and do not worry.
He takes care of us all.
To Him belongs success of any story;
Therefore, just faithfully fulfill your call.

*Saturday 27.06.2020*

# When the sun is rising

When the sun is rising,
When the wind is blowing,
Rejoice because without realizing
You live and feel; without knowing…
That it's so good to breathe,
Such a joy it is to walk;
Amazing is to sneeze!
Wisdom is your kind talk!

With this abundance blessed you are!
Rejoice and pray when you go close or far.

*Monday – Tuesday 02–03.08.2010*

# No blessing in worry

When Jesus was speaking on the mount
Of blessing, did He mention one for worry?
No, He did not in any Gospel account.
Therefore, do not worry; make wise and true your story.

*Saturday 23.05.2020*

# Love God and walk in His ways!

Love God and walk in His ways!
Doing so will prolong your days;
They will be filled with happiness and joy,
You will build and no one will destroy.

Have faith, avoid doubt,
Be positive about things, they will work out!
You are beautiful and strong!
Be courageous all the way along!

*Sunday 17.03.2013*

## Smile and the world will smile with you

Smile and the world will smile with you,
Even your little friend will gently mew.
Don't worry, be happy
And everyone will say, "You're snappy!";

You are free, isn't it cool?
Of course, all this is not a rule,
It's normal to be sad sometimes;
To make you feel more sure is the aim of my rhymes.

*Saturday 07.05.2005*

## Joy (2)

Despite all hardships, remember about joy:
Make time for the good things you enjoy:
Reading, praying, resting, cooking, sleeping, communication;
Keep sober judgement, research, filter information.

*Sunday 03.05.2020*

# The youth of your days

As long as you are young,
Study, achieve all important things, learn a tongue.
Keep faith, be wise when you grow old.
At all times thank God, be bold.

*Sunday 03.05.2020*

# Space for small acts of love

Have space in your life
For small acts of love,
No matter how rough is the strife:
Say a cheerful word, pick up a glove;

Send a smiley over chat;
Be creative, donate a smile;
Lift up your hat;
Share your smart and light style.

*Thursday 13.02.2020*

# Rely on God in what you do!

Rely on God in what you do!
Love your job –
Your work is great, it's true.
Concentrate, you can win, no need to sob!

Pray and go where your heart lies;
Let your spirits rise!
You are a good professional,
Even in the environment which is international!

Rely on God!
Be strong and go –
You can win!
Your work will glow!

*Sunday 30.12.2012*


## Count your blessings

Count your blessings, friend,
Even when there are a few things to amend;
When you lose and when you find;
When things are smooth and when they fall behind.

Count your blessings whatsoever.
Stay kind and clever;
Do your best with the things you've got
When you have little, and when you have a lot.

*Sunday 26.01.2020*


## I know, it is hard if not to say more

I know, it is hard if not to say more,
And you feel tired, indeed.

But you are not alone, for sure –
God is with you, God Who sees your every good deed.

So, come on, cheer up!
Today you can rest,
But tomorrow be quick to get up –
Life is waiting for you to give its best!

*Friday 10.10.2008*


## Success

How to measure success?
By abundant food, bank balance excess;
By driving a sports car;
By exceeding your neighbour's house size by far?

How about having peace with God and inside;
Bringing up your children to respect their family and in faith to abide;
To eat healthy, simple food;
To hope, to love and to be in a good mood?

*Friday 06.12.2019*


## There is a reason for you to be here

Seek the real treasure –
Set out on this adventure.
Through hardships and clear sky azure
May God bless you in your venture.

Perhaps, you will learn
That the perfect gifts are inside;
And the only way to multiply joy is to share it in return.
God loves you and His love will always abide.

*Sunday 01.12.2019*

## Live for today

Live for today.
Let the trouble of tomorrow not disturb;
Let the past remain bland as food without a herb.
Faithfully pray…

*Monday 28.10.2019*

## Dream your dreams

Dream your dreams of the most beautiful hue
And work to make them come true.
Eat your veggies every day;
Be gentle, patient and faithfully pray.

*Thursday 10.10.2019*

## Let your heart be calm

Let your heart be calm and sure
When you do right, kind things;

When you travel by air, sea and when you're ashore –
Fear not evil people's stings.

It is them who are worried or shortly will be, –
But you stay calm and sure;
Keep your heart and mind free
When it is sunny and when it is going to pour.

*Thursday 10.10.2019*


## Never give up the hope

Never give up the hope;
Keep trying for a good thing.
You may need to refine your scope,
But keep in mind the reward that kind deeds are sure to bring.

*Monday 07.10.2019*


## Church rejoicing

Have you ever thought
That a true Christian Church is triumphant indeed?
With all the spiritual fights it successfully fought,
The wisdom it has to feed…

Therefore, let us rejoice
So that when an outsider
Comes and hears our voice,
(S)he should glorify God and wish to become an insider.

*Sunday 15.09.2019*

## Simple acts of kindness

Today I was running late.
The bus driver noticed and waited.
This was a simple act of kindness, what else to state?
I am going to phone his organisation – his deed will be highly rated.

*Thursday 18.07.2019*

## God forgives trespasses

God forgives trespasses
When we sincerely regret and accordingly act.
Therefore, do not look back as the time passes –
Move on with wisdom, humbleness, courage and tact.

*Monday 08.07.2019*

## A new day is a new life

A new day is a new life,
New beginning, new chance
For you, your worker, student, husband or wife,
Therefore, smile and join the dance!

*Monday 08.07.2019*

# Is it raining now?

Is it raining now?
Outdoors or inside?
If outdoors, I make my bow.
The sun will come out for you to go for a ride.

But the latter is complicated.
It has been said a lot,
And much is dedicated
To the word and its plot.

If it hurts inside,
And the soul is longing for light,
Rely upon God in order not to slide.
The pain will vanish,
Your heart will see a wonderful sight.

*Saturday 01.04.2006*


# You live today

Look straight and ahead,
You will wear a crown.
Work with your head,
No need to frown.

Save precious time:
Misleading is the past.
Sour is a lime:
Think, be smart, react fast.

*Wednesday 05.08.2009*

# In such a way

Live in such a way
That nothing overshadows your day
Because you skip good words to say,
Good deeds to do, a long-awaited visit to pay.

You work a lot, but remember to rest;
No need to overwork, just do your best.
In studies, prepare timely for your test.
Say prayers and with love build your nest.

*Friday 05.07.2019*

# Father is so Kind to me

Father is so Kind to me,
He gives me strength,
He makes me sure that I will never flee,
No matter what is the length.

I call on Him and the Father hears.
Hallowed be His Name!
He delivers me from all my fears.
Unsurpassed is His fame!

Our Father in heaven is Kind,
He is Loving and Gracious.
He forgives our debts and no one will find.
Thank Thee, Father, for our freedom is spacious!

*Sunday 16.03.2008*

# Rejoice when it is day and at night!

Rejoice when it is day and at night!
Rejoice in all God's works!
Rejoice for you live and have sight!
Accept with gratitude drops of water and food loaded forks.

*Friday 28.06.2019*


# Helping others will pay off one hundred times

Helping others will pay off one hundred times.
From real life are drawn these lines.

When a creature suffers on this land,
Do not hesitate, give a hand.

If you can help resolve a problem, act.
The soul is too dear to neglect.

Your soul will live, you will thrive.
You will be fresh and truly alive.

Let your help though
Be for those who need it, who will use it to grow.

*Sunday 30.05.2010*

# Rejoice despite all!

Rejoice despite all!
Have faith that you will overcome the wall;
That in front of you, there is an open space.
Pray, believe and wash your beautiful face.

*Sunday 28.02.2013*

# STUDIES & WORK

## Joy (1)

Remember to leave some space for joy
Even if you do not enjoy
All the hard work and studies sometimes,
Even if you get unexpected limes.

Let your heart not be troubled
Or your hardships will be doubled.
Rely on God truly.
Enjoy every moment fully.

*Saturday 26.12.2020*

## Life is changing without a stop

Life is changing without a stop;
Even a bottom can become a top –
All will confirm and no one deny.
So, open your heart, aye.

Too late to improve? It's not true!
We can prove for a fool due:
He will win who is never discouraged to strive,
He is intelligent, wise and alive.

*Sunday 13.05.2007*

## Life, what can be better!

Life, what can be better!
At any point you can rise.
You can write your letter,
You can win your prize.

You can improve all things
Because you are alive.
Stick together; spread your wings!
Birds can fly and fish can dive.

Nothing is irreparably lost
Till life is inside.
Small seems to be the cost;
You will flourish and glide.

Yes, time is incredibly swift,
But life, life is a precious gift.

*Tuesday 31.03.2009*


## Little light

Little light disperses darkness
And drives it away.
Be the light
And let your brightness stay.
If you are unsure where to go,
Shine your way.
May the Lord help your light grow.

*Thursday 17.12.2020*

## Count it blessing and joy

Count it blessing and joy
When you work on different tasks;
When your head and experience are the things you have to deploy;
When you have to sort out multiple asks.

Let patience help you win;
Let discouragement go to a garbage bin;
Let God help you shine the way;
Let your heart continue to pray.

*Thursday 17.12.2020*


## To climb up any hill

We ought to fear God more than men:
He was, He is, and He will be then.
People are and are gone;
Only those, who feared God, won.

Let us not fear to be scared,
But let us fear to do His Will.
Then we can hope to be spared
And to climb up any hill!

*Sunday 29.09.2013*

## Always remember about God

In work and studies it may be tough,
But remember about God, your Saviour, and have faith at all
times –
This will take you out of the water that's rough.
Do your part even when you get limes.

*Sunday 15.11.2020*


## All victories

Victories are from God.
Call and you will win.
Go straight and love.
Let your way be clean and light.

Believe, my friend,
However hard,
Be brave until the end.
Be wise, regard.

*Wednesday – Thursday 07–08.07.2010*


## Just let people feel they are people

Just let people feel they are people,
No matter rich or poor, big or little;
Treat your neighbour as an equal.
Listen, this story has a sequel.

Doing so you'll make them happy,
Your body and soul will be healthy and snappy.
Anyway, you are free to choose,
Decide what is for you, to win or to lose.

You'll ride a horse white,
Your conscience will be clear and light.
You'll be treated the same way in return.
It's always time to learn…

*Monday 25.05.2009*


## Rely on God in every matter

Rely on God in every matter.
You need this to be saved and to succeed;
In order to get slimmer, not fatter;
In order to be wise and not to be in need!

*Thursday 13.06.2013*


## When I eat a lot

When I eat a lot,
I often do a nought.
How strange it is,
But it is with wisdom's breeze!

It is, however, true
That eating nothing is undue.

53

In balance the secret lies,
Stubborn is he who denies.

*Sunday 28.02.2011*


## Do right and money will follow

Do right and money will follow.
Even if not, you will receive.
Your home will not be hollow.
Hot arrows of evil will fail to deceive.

*Friday – Saturday 11–12.03.2011*


## How to win in an argument

The best way to win
In an argument is to avoid it.
Sharp as a shark's fin…
In order not to engage use your wit.

*Sunday 31.03.2013*


## Do not overdo

Do not overexpose yourself, friend:
Avoid trying to please all in the end;
Just do right and keep the Christian peace in your heart;
Be your kind, wise self, be smart.

*Friday 18.09.2020*

## Believe in God and achieve

Believe in God and achieve.
By God's love we will live
It is time to improve, not to leave!
You have so much to give!

*Sunday 06.01.2013*


## Keep calm & work on

Do your best and avoid doubt.
Keep going and looking ahead.
Stop looking back at others to compare if your work is stout.
A hard-working, intelligent and faithful lad will never lack
bread.

*Saturday 29.08.2020*


## Remember to pray

As swift as life may be,
Remember to pray –
It's healthy and free;
It helps keep worry at bay.

*Friday 07.08.2020*

# Avoid hurry

A person who is hurrying is prone to make mistakes;
Therefore, it is wise to spend as much time as it takes.
I do not say be slow,
But avoid unnecessary hurry or you may suffer a blow.

*Sunday 02.02.2020*

# On time

Do important things on time,
If possible, at once, indeed.
This is to help you save a dime
And a lot of effort on a reactive deed.

*Sunday 02.00.2020*

# Time

Time is cunning,
It works when you sleep.
There is no use in running –
Instead be wise, think deep.

No matter how rich you are,
Time is the same for you and the poor.
Who will explain so far,
How to manage time and to endure?

However strange,
The answer is written long ago:
Love God and love your neighbour above any range.
This will direct you on the road to go.

Time continues to move:
It can work for or against you.
Rely on God, be brave, improve.
You will be as if a flower in the freshest morning dew.

*Sunday – Monday 12–13.09.2010*

## Extra effort to win

Sometimes the difference between winning and losing is slight.
Therefore, it is wise to do every little thing right;
To make decisions that are smart
And to work toward the victory from the start.

*Sunday 24.05.2020*

## Remember to smile (1)

Smile and stay agile
To score your goal and be happy too;
Good humour is important, so is cheerful mood;
Pray for all you've got and for each and every day.

*Sunday 31.05.2020*

## Pearls before swine*

Sometimes you may find
Yourself in a situation
Where some don't mind
Giving you hard time for your kind, useful information.

There are, in contrast, those, indeed,
Who can appreciate
And gratefully heed;
Therefore, be wise to differentiate.

* Math. 7:6.

*Wednesday 17.06.2020*

## Life, light, love

What is written in your heart?
Rage and pain or love and care?
In the play, what is your part?
Decide and let your way be fair.

Life is too short to be indecisive, so act –
Who knows when the last day will arrive.
It is both easy and hard, in fact.
Remember this and thrive.

But some people forget
That they are alive
And what makes a soul regret…
I wish they could see where they drive.

Now abide –
And let's try to never let those slide –
Faith, hope, peace dove,
Life, light, love.

*Sunday 01.02.2009*

## Do what's most important first

Do what's most important first
And other things will follow.
Satisfy your knowledge thirst
And choose wisdom to swallow.

*Sunday 02.01.2011*

## Zest & rest

It is important to work with zest –
This is to earn success.
It is also important to rest –
This is to have more energy, not less.

*Sunday 07.06.2020*

## A comfort zone

You need a comfort zone
To be able to go out of it.

Therefore, stay fit.
We all need rest – you are not alone.

*Saturday 20.06.2020*


## Work – rest balance

Don't take your work too seriously, buddy,
But also don't take it too lightly.
The same is true when you study.
Accept what's due – decline other things politely.

There are jobs concerning health and life – true:
At those be vigilant all the way through.
After any job: have family time;
Enjoy rest; read a positive rhyme.

*Friday 12.06.2020*


## Hard work pays off mighty

If you invest efforts rightly,
Hard work pays off mighty.
If you write, study or teach,
Do well and you will reach.

*Friday 29.05.2020*

## How to achieve

Use consistency in important things;
Avoid phone, email and other distraction,
Use the freshness of the day that the morning brings,
Take healthy hydration, exercise, food, sleep action.

*Sunday 31.05.2020*


## Exercise your brain

Exercise your brain
If you want it to gain.
It is like a muscle:
Make it work, avoid hassle.

*Sunday 31.05.2020*


## If you don't know your calling

If you don't know your calling, do not despair;
Deploy persistence and prayer.
Perhaps, your dream job is just an application away...
Keep searching and pray.

*Friday 29.05.2020*

# The days of the week

Monday is a day that is often underestimated,
But is a gift to those whose Sunday was to God dedicated.

Tuesday is the day to follow up with clients and on your
commitments.
To work steady and to help at home with fitments.

Wednesday is the day to keep on going,
To believe, to hope on without knowing.

Thursday is another good day for follow-ups
And to keep positive despite any downs or ups.

Friday is the day to be free in the eve;
To rest and to roll down your sleeve.

Saturday is for all worthy work in the house,
In the garden with your kids and spouse.

Sunday is the day that is to God to be dedicated;
To refocus your mind on the Things that will never become
outdated.

*Friday 08.05.2020*


# When the things are going not the way you'd like

When the things are going
Not the way you'd like,
Do not stop rowing,
Pick up the mike.

The past is in the past.
Proceed with a prayer and hope.
Make conclusions from all the events, both first and last;
Rely on God and go <u>up</u> the slope!

*Saturday 10.05.2014*


## To instructors

You are not a gate keeper, but a guide
To take people through the bridge
From "I don't know and can't" to the "I know and can" side.
Make sure that your style is warmer than a fridge.

Also make sure that you do not slow down
Eager learners on their way;
With slower ones – no need to frown.
Teach all to learn, to work, to play.

*Wednesday 08.04.2020*


## Love God with all your heart, believe in Him and go

Love God with all your heart,
Believe in Him and go!
Defend your thesis, every part.
Be in high spirits, not low!

*Sunday 03.11.2013*

# Persistence

Did you know that many dissertations
Were finished through persistence:
One little step at a time, without any major innovation,
With a lot of focus and family assistance;

With the computer in the airplane mode,
Same with the phone;
With morning hours carrying the core load
Of the day's work; in crowded libraries, but on their own?

How is that related to all?
Persistence and concentration –
Not a big blow – bring down the wall.
To break through, stock up with patience and preparation.

*Sunday 05.04.2020*

# Look up

Try good things, let your dreams come true!
Your kind heart lights up the way.
Try, you <u>will</u> break through,
You will enjoy the day.

Cherish your hope,
It will grow into action.
You and I are strong to cope.
Wisdom will make road to perfection.

*Friday 23.01.2009*

## Come on!

Are you tired? Come on!
Look at others,
So much can be done!
Look at working mothers:
Two jobs, a child and studies.

It is hard, no doubt,
But I say, "Yes, we can".
Try and you will find out –
You can!
To go on and to win is the plan!

*November 2009*

## Rely on God and start all things with a prayer

Rely on God and start all things with a prayer
This will protect you and will help become a soldier, a
professor, a mayor.
Rely on God and do your best.
Devote yourself to the most important things, do not worry
about the rest.

*Sunday 11.05.2014*

## Money is not all

Try to buy a hundred grams of love –
It's harder than to buy a glove.

Try fifty more of happiness and joy –
It is your life, it's not a ploy.

Thank God for this.
This word won't miss.
There are so many things around
You cannot buy, and they abound:

A friend, sunrise, new life,
Warm summer rain, good husband, wife.
All this and then much more.
Thank God, life is not a store.

*Sunday 27.09.2009*


## Love God with all your heart (2)

Love God with all your heart
And other things will follow.
Being loving is a demanding art,
Your house will never be hollow.

*Easter Sunday 05.05.2013*


## Use your smile (1)

Use your smile with confidence in your presentation.
Avoid the grumpiness temptation.
Learn and teach your children to smile
At home and at work to inspire and to cover a mile.

*Thursday 05.03.2020*

# The night is passing

The night is passing,
The day is coming.
Wash your face and be ready,
Continue your work and be steady!

*Friday 29.03.2013*


# Rely on God and be courageous

Rely on God and be courageous in all.
Remember that God not only exists, but loves you, supports –
Just do your part, do not give up the ball –
In studies, work and with all types of cohorts.

*Friday 28.02.2020*


# Have life in yourself

Have life in yourself whatsoever!
They want you to snooze,
But remain active and smart ever.
Pray to God in order not to lose.

Remain kind, be wise.
You should stand, you should not fall;
Your business should be on the rise.
God is above all!

*Sunday 09.12.2012*

# Do Christians need money?

Do Christians need money?
Yes, they do, to pay for bread and honey,
To help those in need
And to accomplish a worthy deed.

But is money the Christian objective?
No, because Christians are selective
About what they pursue:
Faith, hope, love, compassion and other things that are true.

*Wednesday 19.02.2030*


# Simplicity in all

Simplicity is important in all:
Work, sales, reply, studies;
In treating stings;
With ladies and buddies.

If possible, stick to it fast.
In some situations
Add complexity to get past,
But with that, – avoid overuse temptations.

*Monday 20.01.2020*

# There are a lot of things for you to achieve

There are a lot of things for your to achieve,
Be constant in prayer and go!
If you want to receive – believe.
Hardships are necessary for us to grow.

In all things let your light be bright!
Let people see your faith in the eyes and deeds.
You believe and you do right.
To make a good harvest you have to plant a lot of good seeds.

*Sunday 25.11.2012*


# Live and breathe with a full chest

Live and breathe with a full chest,
Of course, when the weather permits.
At work neither underdo nor overdo, just do your best.
Strive for the better and also cultivate your own good bits.

Live and breathe with a full chest;
With love and care build your nest.
As tough as it may be, focus on the good.
Make sure that happiness and joy are biggest in your mood.

*Tuesday – Saturday 06-10.08.2019*

## Protect good things

You have to learn
To defend yourself and yours
Against darts that burn
And an unrighteous talk that blurs
The border of good and bad.
Build and stand your ground.
Whoever gets upset or mad –
Remain bold and sound.

*Friday 10.01.2020*


## Overexposing

Overexposing ourselves may hurt
With bosses, partners, friends –
We may end up in dirt
Instead of shaping rising trends.

Therefore, let us avoid trusting overly to all;
Let us have patience and protect our back;
Let's pay attention in things big and small;
Let us be strong and prepared for a hack.

*Monday 06.01.2020*


## Remember to smile (2)

Remember to smile –
However hard you work or study –

To cover a mile
And to help your buddy.

*Monday 06.01.2020*


## Love God with all your thought

Love God with all your heart
And bravely act!
Let your love be full and not in part,
Let not routine of everyday distract.

You have so many gifts,
Believe and act!
Do honestly your shifts,
But also use wit to promptly react.

*June – July 2012*


## Faith, hope, love (2)

When all things go wrong, keep hope:
God will send you strength to cope.
When you do not know the outcome, believe:
What you want, by Gracious Will you can receive!
When all around turn away, do not abandon love:
We are fighting for the things not below, but above!

*Saturday 01.12.2012*

# Defend your thesis with God's help

No one will defend your thesis, only yourself:
With God's help you can do.
Be not afraid, but be ready.
Let your words be steady!
Let your research be bold and true!
Defend and let it help others and win the best library shelf!

*Sunday 03.11.2013*


# Respect yourself

Start doing good things
And other things will follow.
Doing good will strengthen you wings,
And your pocket will not be hollow!

You can do many things!
No worries about the tree year rings,
Just start!
The big is made of every part!

*Friday 02.12.2011*


# Caution & wit

Use caution and wit to escape
Any misfortune, betrayal and vape.
These will keep you healthy and secure;
You will overcome, you will endure.

*Wednesday 06.11.2019*

## Job search

When you are looking for a thing,
Be persistent, keep on trying
For you never know what the next application may bring.
If you are doing the due diligence and they are not buying,

Do not worry:
God has prepared
For you a better job, company, story
So that your skills should be properly paired.

*Friday 22.11.2019*


## As much as you can, believe

As much as you can, believe, friend!
Let your faith show in deeds:
Work, say, keep silence, be patient, amend.
Help yourself and others – may God bless you in all your needs.

*Sunday 27.10.2019*


## Shine your way and be the light

Shine your way
In the morning, at night, during the day.
Be the light
When there is plenty of room and when it is tight.

*Sunday 27.10.2019*

## Hope and persistence

Keep hope, persist in good,
Whether you are on a plain or in a wood.
There is no trial without relief;
Therefore, focus on light whether you are a clerk or a chief.

*Thursday 17.10.2019*


## Stay bright in any situation

Stay bright in any situation:
When someone is trying to suppress
And when you speak in front of a nation;
Keep it simple, listen more – speak less.

*Monday 07.10.2019*


## Possess yourself

Possess yourself at all times:
When you rejoice and when you get limes;
Continue putting forward your wisdom and light –
Let others be inspired, let all of you enjoy delight.

*September 2019*

## Use your smile (2)

Use your smile often, buddy,
When the streets are lit with light or when they are muddy;
When you win or when you fall;
When you are at work or in a mall.

Doing so will help with others,
And it will help with your own stuff too.
It will encourage your sisters and brothers
To smile and all of you will break through.

*Monday 19.08.2019*


## Never be sorry about little things

Never be sorry
About little things
Or this may cause worry
Which clips your wings.

Instead, be sure
That God takes care of you,
When you are at sea or ashore,
That His love is true.

*Monday 19.08.2019*

## Leave a little space

Always leave a little space
For a miracle in all,
No matter what hardships you face, –
Do your part, do not give up the ball.

*Thursday 12.09.2019*

## When you want to succeed

When you want to succeed,
On God your hope you need to fix!
When you want to cope with greed,
Rely on God; of faith, hope and love produce your bricks!

*Sunday 29.07.2012*

## Never stop improving

Never stop improving,
No need in proving.
Just build upon good stuff;
Learn from failures and that's enough.

*Thursday 15.08.2019*

# Ways to take worry under control

It is nearly impossible to avoid worry,
But it is possible to take it under control;
To prevent health issues and to deserve glory.
Worry is a dangerous beast, it's not a doll.

The way number one is to pray,
In the morning and in the eve,
Without haste and without delay;
It doesn't have to be long, but make sure you believe.

Another way is faith at all times.
God loves you, right?
Act accordingly even when you get limes;
Remember about the Kingdom and focus on light.

*Wednesday 31.07.2019*


# Overcomplicating and oversimplifying

Overcomplicating and oversimplifying
Are similar sins:
The former prevents from worthy and timely trying;
The latter is in the way of long-term wins.

Is balance, then, the way to go?
Yes, it is and more:
Use wit, take time to grow;
Practise decision making, there is no one-size-fits-all door.

*Monday 22.07.2019*

# Control your hunger to achieve

Control your hunger to achieve
Your goals such as catching a bus,
A good mark to receive,
To avoid any extra fuss.

I do not say forget food
Because this stuff is good,
Only be mindful of extras, sizes and what is on the plate
And do not worry if your lunch is five minutes late.

*Monday 22.07.2019*


# Smile to brighten the day

Smile helps build a house,
Work and study each day;
Whether you wear a khaki uniform or a teacher's blouse,
Use it to brighten your day.

*Monday 08.07.2019*


# Work & rest

Mornings are for work and studies;
Evenings are for rest, shopping, movies and books.
Therefore, work with zest and have time for your buddies.
Do sports, relax, get off computer hooks.

*Friday 10.06.2019*

## Believe as much as you can!

Believe as much as you can!
It is easy to believe
When all goes according to your plan,
But you believe even when all the circumstances deceive.

*Saturday – Monday 22-24.06.2019*

## Keep a positive outlook in all

Keep a positive outlook in all.
I do not say, "be fluffy".
Just do not lose a good disposition of your spirit to avoid a fall.
Practise this when all is good and when projects are stuffy.

*Friday 14.06.2019*

## Smile for all occasions

In every business – smile:
At work, in studies, at home;
Even when you are pushing a shopping cart through an aisle;
When you are in a trench or under a dome.

Doing so will brighten your way,
And it will help achieve your goal.
Therefore, practise smile at night and during the day;
When you are at rest and when you are unloading coal.

*Friday 14.06.2019*

# What's your aim?

What's your aim?
Remember and go.
The way of truth brings fame.
Your tree will grow.

*Tuesday 08.06.2010*

# Make hay while the sun shines

Make hay while the sun shines;
Leave for later fun and wines.
I do not say "overwork" –
Just do your best to earn a tasty fork.

*Sunday 12.05.2019*

# Praise

Flowers need water and creativity – praise –
This fights fatigue and helps overcome laze.
Be hearty in your approbation and lavish in support
For every small achievement in work and student's report.

Charles Dickens, Enrico Caruso, Herbert G. Wells truly
Appreciated positive feedback duly;
They used it to grow
Their talents and now their works glow.

Monday 29.04.2019

# God gave us intelligence to use

God gave us intelligence to use –
Make sure, therefore, that you don't lose
Your head in circumstances that are tough;
Also, no matter how smart you are, laugh.

*Sunday 14.04.2019*

# COURAGE

## You are as you are

When you feel low,
And your chin is down,
You can either frown
Or straighten your shoulders and go.

Without looking back,
You can walk your way.
No matter what they think or say –
You can keep to your track.

Please, do not cry,
Just live and love and hope;
Let not things go down the slope.
Use your head to amend, build, fly.

When the time is hard,
You are not alone, believe:
God Almighty will relieve –
You are so strong in this regard.

*Monday 08.06.2009*


## It is worth living the life

It is worth living the life,
Though it may be tough,
Though it may be a strife.
A pleasant sea is often rough.

Problems melt ice from the heart,
You become attentive to others.
It is hard to do good from the start,
But think about hard-working mothers.

Your life can flourish,
You can trim it with love.
With what your heart to nourish?
Be wise as a serpent and harmless as a dove.

*Saturday 27.02.2010*


## How easy it is to fall

How easy it is to fall
And to moan that you are weak,
But to fight and not to surrender at all –
That's what one should seek!

You are young, you are strong:
It's a shame to give up;
Be sure your misfortunes won't last long;
Being clever is a good position to take up.

*Saturday 21.05.2005*


## You are so strong!

You are so strong!
Your heart is so brave!

Anyone can be wrong;
Remember what the Father gave.

Remember because others
Can only dream of it,
Your poor sisters and brothers.
Remember to benefit!

*Friday 06.11.2009*

## God is Stronger than all

God is Stronger than all,
Rely on Him and go.
With Him, you can climb over any wall.
He protects from any foe.

*Sunday 27.04.2014*

## On guard

Let your heart neither fear nor worry,
Even when people are unfair.
Do not hurry with your answer to avoid being sorry;
Be prepared for all: positivity and anger flare.

*Saturday 07.11.2020*

## Believe in God and let your faith pertain

Believe in God and let your faith pertain.
You will achieve your goal,
Unscored it will not remain;
Lack in nothing will know your soul.

*September 2011*


## Even when something doesn't work

Even when something doesn't work,
Keep on trying to achieve.
When you were a child, you could not use a fork…
It is similar with other things – just try and believe.

*Sunday 12.01.2014*


## Trust in God

Trust in God and do not worry;
May your way be faithful truly.
Remember and share God's glory.
Let your hope and love be living fully.

*Saturday 23.05.2020*


## Everything's gonna be all right (2)

Everything's gonna be all right.
I can do it, so can you.

Look around, what a wonderful sight!
Those who hope and try come through.

You have a kind heart;
What a nice smile!
Each day is a start.
Share your gentle, smart and courageous style!

*Wednesday 16.05.2007*

## Love God, believe

Love God and let your love be true!
With love and faith you will come through.
Believe, God loves you to help and deliver from trouble.
For all your losses, you will receive double.

*Sunday 19.01.2014*

## When all hope was gone

When all hope was gone, You saved me.
I did stand and did not flee!
This was not enough in Your eyes:
You blessed Your servant to win

From the beginning of one day
Until another day's sunrise!
May Your servant's praise
Come before Your face today and in later days!

*Sunday 03.03.2013*

# Regardless of what you hear

Regardless of what you hear around,
Keep in sight the common sense,
The Bible, regardless of how convincingly someone may sound;
Be smart and courageous, hence.

*Sunday 26.04.2020*


# How d'you do?

How d'you do?
Everything will be all right!
I am with you.
Show me your smile which is so bright!

Let's stick together – we are a team;
We will, no doubt, break through.
We are on the beam,
And it is true.

So, let's be sure on the way
And never look back.
Let us, instead, believe, work, pray
To thrive like a lily and not to lack.

*Saturday 01.09.2007*

# Let us be brave

Fears with which I used to fear
Do not approach me, not even near,
Because God is my Asylum and my Fort.
Go away from me those who work iniquity and bind the truth
and distort.

What or whom shall I fear:
God loves us, to me it is clear.
Let those who do evil things fear.
To them who believe, God will wipe off every tear.

*June 2014*

# Understand, believe, stand

Understand, believe, stand.
Bright, sage, light.
Today, morning, day.
Example, yourself, sample.

*Wednesday 18.11.2009*

# Cheer up

Cheer up, everything will be all right!
Rely on God and boldly go.
Keep Him in sight.
He loves you and helps you grow!

*Sunday 30.03.2014*

## You are strong without wine

You are strong without wine:
Wine can make people look like swine.
Be strong to say "no".
Be sure, your success will grow.

If you are weak – pray,
Your prayer will be heard that very day.
If you lack wisdom, ask,
You will cope with any task!

*Saturday 12.07.2014*


## You should still remember to smile

You should still remember to smile;
Though, I know, sometimes it's hard;
A kind heart is often fragile,
But look at the sky and the sea, and the yard –
Ain't the view amazingly bright?
Every plant and creature tries to revive;
However cold or hot, they see the light.
Strive.
They are free, they are alive!

*Monday 30.04.2007*

# When it is hard, stand

When it is hard, stand:
Soon, very soon you will see the light.
Believe, just stand!
Your ideas are bright!

Your smile shines…
God will send you warmth and delight!
Believe, you are strong!
Let winning be your song.

*November 2009*

# Keep believing

Whatever happens in your life, keep on believing!
Whatever they say, do not stop dreaming.
The bright day will come.
With love and faith proceed, in sum!

*Sunday 18.05.2014*

# Everything will be all right

Everything will be all right,
But you keep on rowing:
Work during the day, rest at night
For your business to thrive, for your face to be glowing!

*Sunday 01.09.2013*

# Do your part & do not worry

What you can do, do,
But do not worry.
Let God do His part for you.
Do what you can; He is the One Who makes us break through.

*Wednesday 01.04.2020*


# Smile!

Smile and the world will smile with you!
One more day or, maybe, just a few
And all will be all right.
Believe and keep on working towards light!

Cheer up – it all will settle down:
You will see more of green and less of brown;
You will enjoy the fruits of your own work;
You will, certainly, have a plentiful fork!

*Monday – Wednesday 30.06 – 03.07.2014*


# You are a believer

Are you a believer? Yes, you are.
You have the Protector whether you go close or far.
Therefore, do not be afraid, but clever;
Have courage and stay positive ever.

*Thursday 26.03.2020*

## Believe, be constant in prayer

Believe, be constant in prayer;
Whatever happens around,
Let your love and faith, and hope be strong on every layer.
Let your mind be sound!

Whether good or bad,
Believe and hope.
Wash your face, do not be sad:
With prayer you will overcome any hill and any slope.

*Sunday 03.10.2010*


## Have love in yourself and have life

Have love in yourself and have life,
Be courageous, do not be afraid.
Whether you are young or old, a husband or a wife,
You are great, you can succeed in your trade!

*Wednesday 17.04.2013*


## Rely on God and boldly step

Rely on God and boldly step.
Let betrayal, grumpiness, fear not keep you low.
Be wise, assertive and creative
With a newcomer, a visitor, a native.

*Thursday 12.03.2020*

## Love God and be courageous (2)

Love God and be courageous,
Do things with love and hope!
Even if someone is outrageous,
Let not your faith slope.

*Sunday 09.02.2014*

## Your colours

I see your colours shining bright:
In the plain day and in the dark night!
Your light is amazing!
Your way is trial-blazing!

You have an intelligent head –
A lot of literature has been read.
Keep your chin up,
Keep strong in faith, do not give up!

*Sunday 21.04.2013*

## Keep hope whatsoever

Keep hope whatever happens in life,
Whether you are a president, an unemployed or a housewife.
Believe, God will not abandon you!
His blessings are without number. Misfortunes are few.

The sun will shine for you!
You will wash your feet in the morning dew.
But now withstand –
You will receive the Helping Hand!

*Friday 29.03.2013*


## Let your faith be strong

Let your faith be strong,
Let your face be bright!
You will win, although it may take a little bit long.
Have salt in yourself and have light!

*Sunday 04.08.2013*


## To smile

Smile even when hardships are abundant;
Be courageous whatsoever,
Even though the mistakes are redundant.
Simply be clever!

For God is Almighty:
He is your Strength and Support.
He helps you in need,
He drives your ship to a safe port!

*Sunday – Monday 13-14.11.2011*

## Pray and do not worry

Pray and do not worry.
Do what you can at all times.
Believe, however hard is your story.
Keep smiling – remember, we all get limes.

*Sunday 27.10.2019*

## When there seems to be no escape

When there seems to be no escape,
Pray, my friend!
Do not run away from your landscape;
We never know what will be in the end.

Maybe, God has lowered us for an instant
To bring us yet higher at a later time.
Keep on trying although victories seem distant!
Let us pray to make juice of our lime!

*Sunday 20.05.2012*

## Do good with a sincere heart!

Do good with a sincere heart!
Do good from the start
Because we do not know what will happen then,
Only God knows what will happen and when.

Do good today,
No need to delay
Do good when you can do so,
Let kind things grow!

*Sunday 06.05.2012*


## A good soldier

Focus on light and be of good cheer.
Keep and protect the things that are dear.
The support is not far – it's near.
Be a good soldier with faith and honour, without hatred or fear.

*Monday 04.11.2019*


## Useful person

You are not useless even if someone says so;
Even when someone makes it appear that way.
Do you remember how you helped that old lady to mow;
How you brightened your friend's day?

You will hear all kind of things,
But do not listen to all.
Stay away from poisonous stings;
Focus on light and your Christian call.

*Monday 28.10.2019*

## Live and be brave

Live and be brave.
Say kind words, do kind deeds.
You are free, you are not a slave:
Behave as such; plant kind seeds.

*Wednesday – Thursday 16-17.10.2019*


## When life is hard

When life is hard,
Don't worry.
Just be on guard.
Pray. May God make you shine in glory!

*Sunday 12.08.2012*


## With God you will overcome

You have entrusted your ways to God truly,
Therefore, do not worry – only do your part duly.
You will overcome your hardships, son.
God will bless you in all the good things you have done.

*Thursday 26.09.2019*

# I pray

When I want to cry, I pray
And God improves my day!
God fights Himself for His slave!
I only have to be brave.

*Monday 03.12.2012*

# Courageous, witty, happy, healthy, agile

You are the salt
Of the earth, friend;
You are the light of the world.
Avoid despair or finding fault.

Be courageous and witty till the end.
God looks after you when you run and when you sleep curled.
To help in every good deed, use smile.
Be happy and healthy, stay agile.

*Thursday 15.08.2019*

# Believe, amis!

Believe despite hardships, ami(e)!
Whether you like cheddar or brie,
When all is good, remember too:
Faith, hope and love are a must to break through.

*Monday 24.06.2019*

## God gives all (2)

God gives all:
Happiness and health,
With or without wealth;
He also hears when you call.

Be brave, He is with you.
Do good and live.
The time is short, the days are few.
Be brave, kind and wise; when you can, give.

*Sunday 09.01.2010*


## Faith

Regain your faith!
Keep heading forward, my friend,
For the Father grants you strength,
His might and mercy will not end.

*July 2011*


## It's never too late

It's never too late,
Whatever you feel.
Go ahead, what for to wait?
Rust covers resting steel.

When everything seems to be lost,
Start from the beginning.
There is something which is beyond any cost...
The bell of life inside of you is ringing!

It's never too late,
Just try!
What else to state?
Believe, wisdom makes people fly!

*Saturday 22.03.2008*


## Believe despite all bad and good

Believe, although it may be hard –
God more than just exists, –
Be on guard,
Even though someone else otherwise insists.

Believe, God loves and cares.
He helps the one who dares,
The one who loves and hopes
That God will help over pits and slopes.

Believe that with God's help you'll do,
Somehow you will break through.
Have faith and work having rolled up your sleeve;
Despite all bad and good, believe.

*Monday 03.06.2019*

## Be brave to act

Be brave to act
And bravely act!
You will achieve.
Only believe!

*Tuesday 08.06.2010*

## Stand

Whatever happens, stand
Despite all hardships and misfortunes,
Despite your words or deeds you need to amend;
Despite all losses and fortunes.

When it's more than you can handle, pray.
You have the Church, your family and friends, hey!
No need to wait for a negative thing to arrive…
Keep praying and in prayer thank, share, ask – you are alive.

*Tuesday 23.04.2019*

## Life is so good

Life is so good
In spite of failures and slips
That we can't avoid putting to our lips;
But no one is to be always in a bad mood.

We need defeats to realize
How sweet victories are,
To see them, but not from afar.
Life is a pleasant surprise!

*Friday 24.12.2004*

# LET US CELEBRATE TOGETHER

## The most precious gift

The most precious gift is the one of love, for certain,
Whether you are a Quebecois or Albertan;
The gift you share with those in need,
When you help care, or feed…

*Thursday 10.12.2020*


## The essence of Christmas

What is the essence of Christmas, let's think:
Christmas lights, candies, buys,
Eating the whole pudding in a wink,
Winning a monetary prize?

Well, the things above make certain sense,
But they should take no precedénce.
Christ is the centre of Christmas light,
In Him is our peace, freedom, delight.

*Thursday 10.12.2020*


## Christmas values

Big or small, let your Christmas giving be sincere;
Let your Christmas taking be with gratitude truly.
Christ has come – let your way be clear!
May God bless us with peace, faith, hope, love fully!

*Wednesday 09.12.2020*

## Everything's gonna be all right (1)

Everything's gonna be all right,
Because you are so bright.
You are strong as well
And as kind as a Christmas bell!

You have such a loving heart,
No one will change this part.
What a friendly smile!
Thank God for you! Here is no while.

You are so strong
And let it last long!
Believe, all the above is true,
Each letter. All this God has given to you!

*Thursday 08.02.2007*


## Let the sky sing today

Let the sky sing today,
Let the sun shine!
And we are going to pray,
For this is God's day!

*Friday 06.04.2012*

## This day was created by God

Let's be happy today.
We live – it is great!
Other words are needless to say.
Tomorrow can be a bit late.

Yesterday's stuff is in the past.
Our future is being made now.
Be happy, wise and fast.
Remember to smile and do not give up your plough.

*Monday 20.07.2009*


## New year, new day

A new year and a new day
Are a new life
For a wise person: old and young, single and wife.
Therefore, take it easy, improve, thank, pray.

*Saturday 28.12.2019*


## Faith, hope, love (1)

Faith makes all things
Possible, as if you were on wings.

All things are tolerable with hope –
Use it however steep is the slope.

Love makes all things ideal:
Make sure it is living and through deeds is real.

Let none of these three above be blind.
Be gentle, courageous and wise;
Seek true things and you will find.

*Wednesday 18.12.2019*

## What does a linguist need for Christmas?

This is a good question.
A crossword, perhaps, can be a suggestion;
A dictionary or a mouthful of words;
Review with him/her his/her linguistic awards…?

A good linguist, listen, o friend, –
If s/he does not pretend –
Needs, as we all do,
Faith, hope and love that are true.

*Thursday 19.12.2019*

## How was your Christmas?

How to measure how well your Christmas was truly?
By how much Christ there was in it;
Whether or not you shared Christmas joy fully;
Whether you used and shared your gifts with wit.

*Thursday 12.12.2019*

## Christmas joy

What is Christmas joy?
It is our hope
That every girl and every boy
Has the Helper to cope

With every hardship and fatigue;
To join the brightest league;
To accomplish good deeds
And to remove from their heart all weeds.

Christ has come
To help us on our way:
Let us be thankful and faithfully pray.
Believe, you are loved and can overcome!

*Thursday 12.12.2019*


## New year

What is the importance of a new year?
It gives us an additional chance to share hope and care;
To sum up the passing time;
To show love to our neighbour in deeds and to donate a dime.

*Thursday 12.12.2019*

## St. Nicholas

Did you know that Santa Claus, indeed,
Is Sinterklaas who is, in turn, St. Nicholas who helps in need?
Unlike in popular culture, however,
This person is not all "fluffy", but has kept his personality ever.

He knew a poor man –
To help him and his three daughters was St. Nick's plan.
His presents went a long way.
St. Nicholas still helps and gives presents by the way…

*Wednesday – Thursday 18-19.12.2019*

## Hiding place

Have you ever thought
That the Church can be a hiding place
For all who sought,
For a novice and an ace,

Especially on Sundays and feast days?
It keeps us busy
And to sin we are deprived of ways.
Therefore, have time to stop by and take it easy.

*Monday 08.04.2019*

# MISCELLANEOUS

## How important it is to remember

How important it is to remember
How much you are given:
Eyes and ears, feet and hands and every member;
And though your way is winding, but it's even.

I know, sometimes it's really hard,
And no one seems to understand;
Your own self is difficult to guard,
But keep on rowing, it's closer than you think, the land.

"The darkest hour is before the dawn",
Wisdom says.
So, keep on doing good; with a loving heart you were born.
Kind people are brightly shining rays!

*Sunday 16.09.2007*


## While the sun shines

While the sun shines,
Do good.
Then night comes and day declines –
It will be fast as twilight in a wood.

Do good while you have strength to:
Don't put it off;
The time is fast, oh how much it is true.
Be mindful of cultures, as written by Sapir, Whorf, Lakoff.

*Saturday 10.09.2011*

# Behave

Behave in such a way
That your good consciousness does not condemn you.
Walk during the day;
Stick to what is true.

*Thursday 25.09.2011*

# When in doubt

When in doubt,
Support the weak:
Your muscle is stout,
Your wit is at peak.

Don't be afraid –
Fear does not make us ideal.
Remember the things for which you have prayed.
May God help you make them real!

Do not put it off till tomorrow,
Ask the Father for good things to achieve:
He gives for free – no need to borrow;
Be wise, active, courageous, believe.

*Wednesday 20.04.2011*

## You refused to listen so many times

You refused to listen so many times.
For you to remember are given these rhymes.
Your mother, she always did her best,
All for you till the rest.

Being a boy you were a hero.
She asked in return as much as zero.
Her loving eyes were sleepless for you,
Your ears are open to hear, it's true.

Keep it all in your heart.
Remember she gave you her part.

*Tuesday 19.05.2009*


## Victories

All real victories are from God truly.
Stick to Him with your heart and mind fully.
Observe His commandments in words and deeds.
He is the One Who supports, frees and feeds.

*Sunday 29.11.2020*


## A greedy person hopes to save

A greedy person hopes to save,
But becomes a slave.

Trying to make rich his/her door,
Greed loses all, even more.

First, come little things;
Then money, gold, expensive rings.
A bit later – health and friends;
At last, love and life and greed ends.

*Monday – Saturday 26–28.05.2007*


## If you are thirsty, come and drink

If you are thirsty, come and drink,
God has enough water for all.
Do not give up reason, think!
To get answers, consider this call.

If you are hungry of truth, come and eat,
God is the Bread of Life; you will live, you won't retreat!

*Sunday 23.06.2013*


## Save yourself

Save yourself and thousands will be saved beside you:
It is a strange thing, but it is true.
Believe, my friend, and abide in faith.
Every new day is for you to bathe:

Wash your face, you are an example to others;
You can help save your sisters and brothers.

Stay strong in faith and believe;
Be patient, work for your reward, receive.

*Sunday 14.04.2013*

## One may want to lead you astray

One may want to lead you astray.
Watch out!
Others will try to show you the way.
Keep the line, be stout.

Let your aim be always in view.
The wind will blow,
But the morning will bring fresh dew;
You will see the sun glow.

Our part is small, in fact:
To do all we can,
Trust in God; be smart, react.
To win in spite of all is our plan!

*Saturday 13.09.2008*

## Oh Gracious God

Oh Gracious God, deliver me from the evil
And from my own self protect;
Obedience to You in studies and things civil
Direct my heart to select.

For I want to glorify
My Creator and God in all.
Fortify my soul
And in need, hear my call.

*Sunday 28.04.2011*


## Choose a healthy life

If you live in a place,
Where pesticides or herbicides are used on a lawn:
Alas, my friend – just make healthy at least your space,
Do not worry, be the healthy example from rise to dawn.

*Friday 18.09.2020*


## Have power to master your body and soul

Have power to master your body and soul.
Being patient is the start;
Remember your goal.
Rely on God, from this point depart.

*Saturday 05.03.2011*


## The pandemic: Wearing a mask

It may stink;
It may not be pretty,

But it prevents spread of germs that happens in a wink.
If not for yourself, wear it for others, be witty.

*Tuesday – Friday 08–11.09.2020*

## Have life

Have life in yourself,
Not as old dust on the shelf.
Be active and smart,
Both outside and in your heart!

Let your light
Shine all misfortunes in spite.
Maybe, not all things were right,
But keep the most important thing in sight!

*Sunday 24.03.2013*

## A currency

A smile is important in studies;
In dealing with customers, vendors and buddies.
Feel free to share a sincere one with others:
Colleagues, friends, children, parents, sisters and brothers.

*Saturday 29.08.2020*

## You are longing for peace

You are longing for peace,
But the whole world seems to be going wrong.
Walk your way, do not cease.
Soon you'll hear the winning song.

*Tuesday 03.03.2009*


## To rise is to live

It isn't so bad to fall,
But it is bad not to get up.
Mistakes are known to all;
So, find the will to stand up.

The world is big,
The aims are many;
A spade is made to dig,
And cement is made to seal a cranny.

You may fall, but rise
For people to admire!
Fall and rise…
For perfect love and life entire!

*Wednesday 18.02.2009*

116

## Pride precedes a fall

Pride precedes a fall:
Be ready to withdraw.
To be wise is my call,
To save and not to break the last straw.

But be courageous, my friend;
Let your enthusiasm remain.
Be persistent in good; eat your bread.
Keep faith, be sane.

*Friday 02.04.2011*


## No one knows what it's like

No one knows what it's like
To feel what I feel.
Good intentions meet a counterstrike,
But time, they say, does heal…

So many things to learn,
The world is weird:
Even water can burn.
Trifles should never be feared.

What shall I do to be wise?
To hit the balance in working and resting, speaking and being
mute.
Silent and gracious is morning rise.
Happy and calm babies are – how much they are cute!

*Saturday 09.08.2008*

# Fear does not help us perfect

Fear does not help us perfect.
So, try to find your balance.
Your relations should be out of its effect;
Be brave to take your chance.

Love will conquer fear!
Believe in God and act.
Save what to our heart is dear.
Be brave and be wise to react.

*Tuesday 28.12.2010*


# Remain yourself

The world will try to change you,
But you remain the one you are.
Your kind heart is true,
Your way will stretch so far!

Remain yourself whatsoever:
They will try to push someone aside.
God's will will last forever;
He wins whose heart is brave and mind is wide.

*Tuesday 03.08.2010*

## Do good

Do good and do not mind
What others think.
Your task is to be kind,
To good things you are a link.

Let your light
Shine to others,
You do right
To your sisters and brothers.

*Sunday – Sunday 05–19.06.2011*


## While travelling

Life is like a travel.
Presently here, a moment later there,
And each day is like a new level.
It's a constant move with stops so rare;

And only those will reach,
Who travel with an aim.
They will learn, and they will teach.
Always in motion and wiser, but never the same.

*Wednesday 14.03.2007*

## When you feel sad

When you feel sad,
Remember: you are not alone.
The situation may be bad,
But you look forward ahead, not back on the phone.

*Sunday – Tuesday 26–28.12.2010*


## A little

You watch TV a little, you nap
And your poverty may come in a snap.
I do not say, "don't rest" –
Be organized, just do your best.

*Saturday 23.05.2020*


## Brief and beautiful

If you have good stuff to share,
Be mindful that the more you write, the less they read.
Therefore, write to the point and beautifully, without glare.
Let percentage-wise they follow more, not less and let them
heed.

*Friday 29.05.2020*

## Much is said – little is done

Much is said – little is done.
Still there, but the time is gone.
There is no use in despair.
The Good knows how to repair.

So, the good is still ahead –
No matter what's been said;
We'll stand again to win and regain.
We strive for a better future again.

*Tuesday 24.02.2009*

## Do not put off important things

Do not put off important things
For only God knows how much time we have truly;
Cherish every moment and invest into life and what it brings;
Believe, have faith, love fully.

*Monday 01.06.2020*

## Remember who you are

In summer glare and winter frost
Remember who you are
And stand your post:
Read the Scripture and let your deeds be up to par.

*Friday 29.05.2020*

## What you give you get back

What you give you get back,
Who can object, for it is wise?
You'll get more than a double size,
Listen in order not to be off the track.

It isn't worth it being shy to give,
I hope that some will understand
And see, and feel where we stand
In order to succeed, to thrive, to live.

To give is to gain,
And it's good and healthy for you.
Just wait and soon you'll get your due,
Be wise and you'll never plain.

*Saturday 14.05.2005*


## By their fruit

Prophets are known by their fruit,
So are professionals, friend.
You have to look into the root
And to analyze the work they send, the trend, the end.

*Sunday 26.04.2020*

# Chasing wrong things

Sometimes we chase wrong things in life.
The point is: however bitter is the strife, –
Have faith to refocus on what is true:
Faith, hope, love which God has meant for you.

*Saturday 25.04.2020*


# Do good as long as you can

Do good as long as you can.
Your remuneration is ready.
You well began.
Your steps will be steady.

Do good, do not refrain:
Your house will be strong;
In the due season you will have rain;
You will live long.

Do good to help your neighbour –
For God helps us too.
Believe, He will lighten your labour.
You will break through.

*Sunday 28.07.2013*

## With God in life

You are not meaningless to me,
That's why I am going to speak.
Please, listen to what I am saying to thee,
Let's listen to be strong, not weak.

Let God live in your mind and soul.
He is knocking at your door;
He doesn't want you to fall in a hole;
He fights for you to move you fore.

Be generous, polite and kind all the way through.
Let God deal with what some people do
Because hate in your heart can consume you too.
Be committed to things that are true.

Be wise, but nice to others:
Help with heavy bags;
Protect babies and mothers;
Help people regardless of flags.

*Saturday 19.11.2011*


## The more you give, the more you get

The more you give, the more you get.
However simple it is, this may be hard to understand.
Only faith can, if you intend to let:
It is your heart that fills your hand.

This is from God and seems strange to us.
Children know this,

124

And you can hear this on a bus.
Open you heart in order not to miss.

*Sunday – Monday 13–14.11.2011*

## If a poem

If a poem helps refocus on a good, positive note for a moment
fully:
Courage, faith, hope, love, work, studies, a smile;
It deserves applause truly;
Use it for positivity and to stay agile.

*Sunday 12.04.2020*

## Love God and be courageous (1)

Love God and be courageous!
Do your work; be simple, wise:
Even if you meet personalities who are outrageous,
Let the sun of kindness and self-possession always rise!

*Sunday 17.11.2013*

## Help and save us

Help and save us,
Father, and help us avoid fuss.

Our days are short,
But send us Thy mighty support.

Please, let us sing praise
To Thee in all ways.
Let our illness be cured,
And what must be, let it be endured.

*Saturday 18.07.2009*


# Be faithful

Don't get upset,
The things will clear in due time.
Be courageous and smart, do not fret.
With faith, hope and love complete your climb.

*Sunday 05.04.2020*


# Do not fear what they are going to say

Do not fear what they are going to say,
Do what should be done, – do kind things.
Do not put off, do them while you are young, while it is day.
Do all you can, but above all – pray.

*Saturday – Monday 14–16.06.2014*

## Drink water

Drink water all the time:
At any season, any period of day.
Drink enough water with and without a lime;
Drink water at work and at play.

Do not rush to food to eat,
But approach water to drink.
This should help if you have set an aim to meet.
Water is an essential health link.

*Saturday 12.04.2014*


## When all seems to go wrong

When all seems to go wrong,
It may only be today.
Misfortunes will not stay long,
The sun will show up for children to play.

But today be strong.
Be wise and wait.
Do not haste with your song –
Today prepare your plate,

You will fill it tomorrow.
Prepare, your day will come.
There is a time to lend and a time to borrow.
Prepare and focus on how strong your success will become.

*Sunday 26.09.2010*

## When the sky is grey

When the sky is grey
And the clouds seem to have covered it all,
Remember, there will be a bright day!
Life is an ocean and problems are small.

Be sure, you will overcome,
I am sure you will do,
You will pick your plum!
Wisdom is calling for you.

*Sunday 30.09.2007*


## Be sure in doing good

Be sure in doing good.
Do not worry if people consider you rude.
Your cause is right.
Your heart and your head are bright!

*Sunday 13.10.2013*


## Believe

If life gives you a lime,
Don't get discouraged, believe!
Just for a little more time!
Be aware of those people who try to deceive.

*Sunday 26.05.2013*

## Your faith

Depend not on what people will think,
Just do the right thing, let your wisdom blink.
Let your faith help be kind.
Love God and your neighbour in deeds and in mind!

*Sunday 30.06.2013*

## Kind deeds (1)

Let all the peoples know:
South, north, east and west,
The truth will grow.
We'll do our best.

We will never keep lukewarm our heart,
We won't get tired.
We'll make a good start:
Our kind deeds will be admired.

*May 2009*

## When your body is healthy, it's good

When your body is healthy, it's good –
Your soul will be sound as well,
You will be in a good mood.
Open your heart, let wisdom tell.

Neither too left nor too right,
But balance.
Your eye will see a magnificent sight
In balance.

Find the measure –
That is the key.
You will feel genuine pleasure,
You will be like a green tree.

*Wednesday 17.06.2009*


## Health tips, not a prescription

Here are a few tips, dude,
That some people use for prevention:
Raw honey, a little of fresh garlic well chewed;
Some lemon, green tea – an old invention;

Washing hands without laze:
With soap and water that's tolerably warm;
Less sugar, more sleep, sun rays,
Rest, fresh air, good hydration to better perform.

These things in measure are easy to use.
They may work or they may not;
Therefore, they must not be an excuse
For not seeing a doc to help with that you've got.

*Honey in any form must NOT be given to infants (babies under one year old). All the other things mentioned should only be tried IF they are clearly safe and are in safe quantities for the intended individuals; to confirm that all the things are safe, speak to your medical doctor in advance.

*Saturday – Sunday 07-08.03.2020*

## Let misfortunes not discourage your heart

Let misfortunes not discourage your heart.
Have fire in you which you had from the start!
Use difficulties to learn
And in the future much more to earn!

*Friday 29.03.2013*

## Kind deeds (2)

Remember kind deeds of your youth.
You are the same kind person – this is the truth.
But your kind deeds now should exceed those in the past.
Your persistence in good should last.

*Thursday 28.03.2013*

## Food

Food should not distract –
It should help you react.
Food should not be the aim –
It should be the means; in it there is no shame.

*Sunday 02.09.2012*

# Be sure, do not hesitate

Be sure, do not hesitate,
No doubt, you will succeed!
Come on, it is never too late,
Smile, don't cry, there is no need.

You will overcome all.
Look forward, do not glance back!
Love will prevent from a fall,
You will suffer no lack!

*Monday 25.06.2007*


# Money as a servant for good deeds

Money is a good servant, indeed,
But a bad master.
Therefore, use it for every good deed
And to help your neighbour faster.

*Wednesday 19.02.2020*


# To softies

Friends, keep kind things as your orientation;
In faith, hope, love, – stay firm.
Have heart of flesh among population;
Keep mind clear and hands without a germ.

*Thursday 22.08.2019*

## Like an eagle your youth will renew

Like an eagle your youth will renew
Because the Lord has become the Refuge for you.
Others will stare,
But you go and God's work declare.

*Sunday 02.02.2020*


## A real softie

Who are real softies indeed?
They are humble and gentle truly;
They are firm in good and kind deed;
They work and help others fully.

*Thursday 22.08.20129*


## How to change the world

The only way to do so
Is to share one good deed at a time
In slow and fast life flow,
Through rhyme, smile and dime.

*Saturday 11.11.2012*

## Margaritas ante porcos*

Helping others is a noble feat:
It may help your friend avoid defeat;
It may fulfill your Christian duty;
It may win you a beauty…

Yet, help must go only where it is needed –
To those who have pleaded.
Therefore, use judgement and prayer
To discern who, when, how and where.

* Lat. for "pearls before swine" (from Math. 7:6).

*Sunday 17.11.2019*


## How to help your digestion & to sleep well

Take good deeds and grind them into fine powder, –
No need to brag about them louder.
Use a spoonful before, at or after a meal;
Be a good Christian with faith, hope, love and zeal.

*Thursday 12.12.2019*


## True colours

Let your true colours shine through.
Laugh with cheer and respect, smile enough.
Take courage when you study, work or cross a lake.
Let your love be not blind, but let it be true.

*Tuesday 12.11.2019*

# A "donkey"

Have you ever thought that your body, indeed,
Is a "donkey" carrying you to the Kingdom of God and your task is to feed
And to take care for it in a proper way:
To prevent a disease, to get enough sleep, to pray…

If you overfeed it, it will go mad;
If you underfeed, it will go bad;
If it gets sick, it will carry no more.
Therefore, be smart and care to reach the Door.

*Monday 02.12.2019*

# Second chance

I believe that we all get a second chance
In all good things: fair business, life, romance.
Although it may seem incidental, thank and believe.
Improve, thrive, receive.

*Monday 07.10.2019*

# Quaecumque vera*

Smile is better than crying;
Courage is better than fearful air;
The truth is better than lying;
Wit is better than a tough head;
Being calm is better than being mad.

Therefore, give up what's worse, choose what's better instead.
Hope is better than despair.

\* Latin for "whatsoever things are true" (Phil. 4:8).

*Wednesday – Saturday 06-09.11.2019*

## Lucky

We are lucky to live, to move, to see;
Above all, we are lucky to love and to be loved truly.
Let us be thankful, let us not flee;
Let us stand, be smart and believe fully.

*Saturday 26.10.2019*

## Wisdom is what I need

Wisdom is what I need.
Resolution is what I lack.
Hesitation is sad, indeed:
One step forward, one and a half back.

Where is right?
What is wrong?
I want to see light.
But sad is my song.

The escape is close, I know.
The key is somewhere inside.

My work is to row.
Let ideas be broad, the world is wide.

*Thursday 23.10.2008*

## Communication

Communication is a sacrifice
That is pleasant to the Lord.
To speak to a person who needs it, to share your rice
Are the things that most of us can afford.

*Wednesday 04.09.2019*

## In what is real pleasure?

In what is real pleasure?
In lots of money or much ice-cream?
In dreaming, constant leisure?
In letting out inner steam?

Trying to answer the question, which is the same:
Where is real pleasure?
Again and again…
It is in finding measure.

*Tuesday – Wednesday 28-29.04.2009*

# Life is passing so fast

Life is passing so fast
Days are running ahead.
Sooner or later, we'll feel at last.
The colour is green, but it's changing to red.

'Watch your time',
I say to myself.
Life can be both honey and lime;
Time won't lie on a shelf.

So, I'd better be quick to perform.
Trifles are cutting my line.
I'd better be wise to bear a storm.
Wisdom makes every day really fine.

*Friday 15.08.2008*


# Sail Day

Today in the Church we had a sail day.
It is not when we get a discount,
But an uplifting opportunity, to gather with like-minded people
to pray;
To say "forgive me", to commune, to do all things that really
count.

*Monday 26.08.2019*

# The sun shines and then comes rain...

The sun shines and then comes rain...
I don't know when I'll be put to the touch.
I only know God loves me much,
I hope to show it's not in vain.

*Friday – Saturday 17-18.03.2006*


# Churching

Have you tried churching, friend?
It is like hiking, but you need to attend
A Church in the countryside or in town.
For this, you may need to walk or to take a ride
And to change to smile your frown.

The key is: that's a spiritual adventure
To help you succeed in every good venture
And to get adequate rest;
To help focus on the important things
And to pass any good test.

*Monday 12.08.2019*


# If your feelings abound

If your feelings abound,
Use a canvas or a rhyme;
Use sports or a walk around –
It's free, no need to spend a dime.

However, posses yourself at all times.
For God is God of order;
Therefore, keep control despite all limes,
When you are at home, and when you cross a country border.

*Sunday 24.06.2019*


## A scientific perspective

Have you ever thought
How man is made:
How countless cells are built together from naught;
How carefully the organs are laid?

Was it possible that cells themselves agreed
That they would stick together to cope with any need?
Or did the brain existed by itself and one day
It said to the stomach, "Hey,
Let's work together, bud!"
And they found the feet to step over any mud?

No, this was not possible at all
As cells have no ability
To communicate enough or call;
And organs are a subject to a high fragility.

So, did this happen by chance?
Shall we adopt an unscientific stance?
This complexity is so immense
That even the brightest of us all together have nothing to say in
their defense.

It only makes perfect sense
When we think of the Creator Who loves, cares and directs to
enhance.

*Monday 10.06.2019*


## The truth

Testify to the truth
And do not worry about things.
Be faithful as Ruth
And help spread people's wings.

*Thursday 20.06.2019*


## Where there is God, there is victory

Where there is love which is true,
There is truth and God indeed.
Where there is God, there is victory all the way through.
It is in word, in thought and in deed.

Only make sure that your love is not blind,
But patient, forgiving, orderly truly.
On God, your neighbour, the truth set your mind;
With that you will win, you will overcome duly.

*Monday 27.05.2019*

# Nonverbal communication

Nonverbal communication is a secret code.
Discover to understand
People's way on the road.
Note what they say with their eye and hand.

Nonverbal cues are a part of conversation;
They show what people like and dislike;
They reveal reliability and importance of information;
Like a thunder they strike!

*Monday 12.07.2010*


# Is the sun still shining bright?

Is the sun still shining bright?
Let's go and check a weather site.
Because there is no more desire
To live, live real, there is no fire!

Does love still exist?
"Oh, yes!!!", postcard companies insist,
"Oh, yes!!!", jewellers support,
"Just purchase, buy; the time is short!"

Has Jo turned off reason?
Has gotten used to indifference and treason?
Perhaps, in this Jo found pleasure...
Alone all day, almost blind by a screen, Jo's "sacred treasure"...

But eyes are to see –
Jo's soul is free.

Ears are to hear –
Jo will change and win, no need to fear!

*Sunday 24.02.2008*


## Sometimes when I write

Sometimes when I write
I feel that it's already been written,
Who's wrong and who's right?
All the records seem to be beaten.

Yes, I don't invent new words,
I just fill them up with my thoughts,
They are free and light like birds;
Now I know they are different as stones and forts.

*Tuesday 19.08.2011*


## The ice will melt

The ice will melt,
The spring will arrive!
For now tighten your belt,
Your life will thrive!

Be sure, take it easy,
You'll have a good job,
Your way will never be sleazy,
Laughter will replace any sob.

Be ready because all will soon change,
Just do not stop trying.
With God's help you can arrange,
You'll be like a bird, singing and flying!

*Sunday 02.12.2007*


## When everything goes wrong

When everything goes wrong,
Do not get discouraged.
You will hear a victorious song,
By God you will be encouraged!

*Tuesday 19.08.2011*

# Index (tags)

145

| | |
|---|---|
| **love** | 2, 4, 6, 9, 11, 12, 13, 14, 15, 16, 17, 18, 19, 20, 21, 22, 23, 24, 25, 26, 27, 28, 29, 31, 32, 33, 35, 36, 37, 39, 41, 42, 46, 52, 55, 57, 58, 59, 63, 65, 66, 67, 68, 69, 71, 75, 76, 77, 82, 83, 85, 86, 88, 90, 92, 93, 98, 100, 103, 104, 105, 106, 107, 109, 111, 112, 116, 118, 121, 123, 125, 126, 129, 132, 134, 136, 139, 141, 142; |
| **mother** | 25, 65, 83, 111, 124; |
| **praise** | 1, 3, 6, 7, 31, 32, 80, 86, 126; |
| **presentation** | 66; |
| **smile** | 14, 23, 27, 28, 38, 39, 44, 57, 66, 70, 75, 78, 79, 86, 87, 89, 90, 91, 94, 95, 98, 104, 105, 115, 125, 132, 133, 134, 135, 139; |
| **studying** | 1, 8, 15, 39, 44, 46, 49, 52, 60, 65, 67, 68, 70, 78, 79, 80, 113, 115, 125, 134; |
| **thanks** | 1, 2, 3, 4, 5, 6, 8, 9, 10, 14, 16, 17, 18, 23, 25, 28, 32, 34, 35, 39, 46, 66, 101, 104, 105, 107, 135, 136; |
| **wisdom** | 6, 8, 12, 13, 15, 24, 25, 31, 35, 37, 39, 43, 44, 49, 52, 53, 54, 56, 57, 58, 59, 64, 67, 74, 83, 89, 92, 99, 100, 105, 106, 109, 110, 117, 118, 119, 120, 122, 124, 125, 127, 128, 129, 136, 138; |
| **word** | 3, 13, 16, 19, 24, 27, 35, 39, 45, 46, 66, 72, 97, 101, 105, 106, 111, 141, 143. |

# Reader's notes

Lightning Source UK Ltd.
Milton Keynes UK
UKHW021838170621
385713UK00002B/495